D1061173

20.99

SPORTS
ALL-ST★RS

GIANNIS ANTETOKOUNMPO

Jon M. Fishman

Lerner Publications ◆ Minneapolis

Lerner Publications Company
A division of Lerner Publishing Group, Inc.
241 First Avenue North
Minneapolis, MN 55401 USA

For reading levels and more information, look up this title at www.lernerbooks.com.

Main body text set in Albany Std 15/22. Typeface provided by Agfa.

Library of Congress Cataloging-in-Publication Data

Names: Fishman, Jon M., author.
Title: Giannis Antetokounmpo / Jon M. Fishman.
Description: Minneapolis : Lerner Publications, [2019] | Series: Sports All–Stars |
    Includes bibliographical references and index. | Audience: Ages: 7–11. | Audience:
    Grades: 4 to 6.
Identifiers: LCCN 2017052355 (print) | LCCN 2017047851 (ebook) |
    ISBN 9781541524606 (eb pdf) | ISBN 9781541524521 (library binding : alk.
    paper) | ISBN 9781541527980 (paperback : alk. paper)
Subjects: LCSH: Antetokounmpo, Giannis, 1994—Juvenile literature. | Basketball
    players—United States—Biography—Juvenile literature. | Milwaukee Bucks
    (Basketball team)—History—Juvenile literature.
Classification: LCC GV884.A56 (print) | LCC GV884.A56 F57 2018 (ebook) | DDC
    796.323092 [B] —dc23

LC record available at https://lccn.loc.gov/2017047851

Manufactured in the United States of America
1-44528-34778-4/5/2018

CONTENTS

THE GREEK FREAK

Giannis Antetokounmpo moves past a Toronto Raptors defender in a 2017 playoff game.

Milwaukee Bucks fans call Giannis Antetokounmpo the Greek Freak. The first part of the nickname is obvious. Antetokounmpo was born in Greece and lived there until he joined the National Basketball Association (NBA) in 2013. They call him Freak because his basketball skills are way beyond normal.

Antetokounmpo showed all of his skills in the **playoffs** against the Toronto Raptors. The Bucks and the Raptors were playing in Milwaukee on April 20, 2017. In the first quarter, a Raptors player took a shot. Antetokounmpo was ready.

Antetokounmpo dunks the ball in the second half of the game against the Raptors.

He soared and swatted the ball away for a **block**. Later, he passed to teammate Thon Maker. Maker sank a basket, and Antetokounmpo was credited with an **assist**.

As the game went on, Antetokounmpo scored baskets and made more assists. He grabbed **rebounds** and raced around the court to steal the ball. The Raptors couldn't keep up. The score at the end of the game was Milwaukee 104, Toronto 77.

Antetokounmpo's stats show what a good all-around player he is. He had 19 points, eight rebounds, four assists, two steals, and two blocks in the game. The win gave the Bucks a lead in the series, two games to one.

As usual, Antetokounmpo had a great time on the court. And he gave some of the credit for the win to the loud crowd. "It was just fun, fun to play with such great fans," Antetokounmpo said. "Hopefully they can show some love and be loud in Game 4."

Unfortunately for Bucks fans, Toronto won the next three games to win the series. But the 2016–2017 season had been a great year for Antetokounmpo. He proved that he has the skill to make the Bucks winners.

The Milwaukee Bucks have existed since the 1968–1969 NBA season. They won the NBA Finals two years later. In 1973–1974, they lost the NBA Finals, and they haven't been back to the championship series since then.

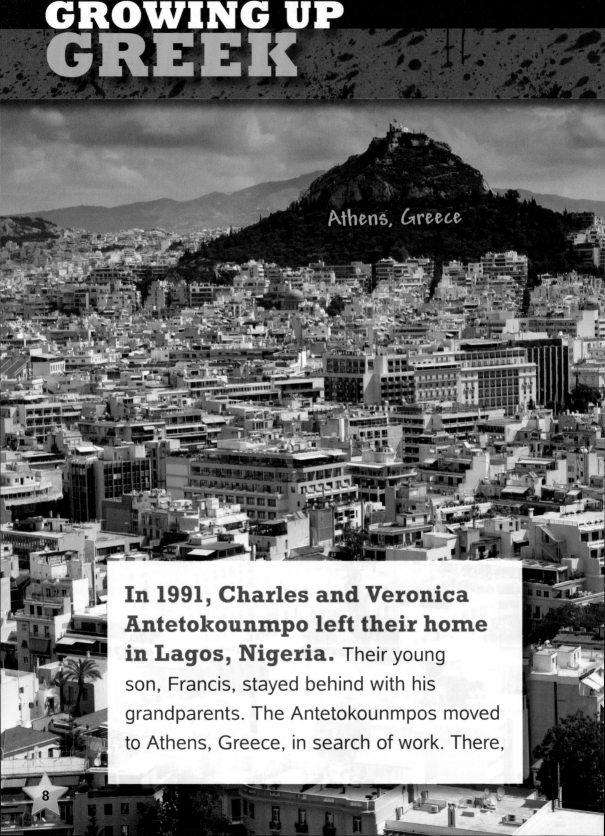

GROWING UP GREEK

Athens, Greece

In 1991, Charles and Veronica Antetokounmpo left their home in Lagos, Nigeria. Their young son, Francis, stayed behind with his grandparents. The Antetokounmpos moved to Athens, Greece, in search of work. There,

Giannis (*right*) stands with his brother
Thanasis at an event in 2015.

they had four more boys: Thanasis, Giannis, Kostas, and
Alex. Giannis was born on December 6, 1994.

Greece had more jobs than Nigeria, but that didn't
make it easy for the Antetokounmpos to find work. They
had arrived in the country without permission. That
meant it was against the law for them to stay. The family
lived in constant fear of being caught. "At any moment,
the [police] can stop you and say come over here and let
me send you back to your country," Giannis said.

His parents picked fruit on farms. They also sold things on the street in Sepolia, the neighborhood of Athens where they lived. The children helped them make money. Giannis and his brothers sold purses and sunglasses. They exchanged beads, toys, and video games. They sold whatever it took to earn enough money to buy food.

Giannis learned valuable lessons on the streets of Sepolia. He became good at reading people. He couldn't waste time talking to people who weren't going to buy something from him. He also learned that no matter how hard he worked, some days he wouldn't earn enough money to eat.

Giannis played basketball while visiting Sepolia in 2015.

Basketball was different. When Giannis worked hard on the court, he always got good results. The sport was an escape from the daily struggle to survive. Giannis spent a lot of time on basketball courts, and people in the neighborhood noticed. "I always knew Giannis was going to be a big deal," neighbor Dimitris Matsagas said. "He lived his childhood on that basketball court."

Giannis also liked soccer, the sport his father preferred. But one day, a basketball **scout** named Spiros Velliniatis spotted Giannis playing on a basketball court with two of his brothers. Giannis was tall and moved with grace. Velliniatis knew right away that the boy could be a special player.

Giannis continues working hard to improve every day as a professional player.

Giannis poses for a photo after the
Milwaukee Bucks chose him in 2013.

Velliniatis convinced Giannis to take the sport seriously. With the scout's help, Giannis began playing **pro** basketball in Greece. Before long, NBA scouts noticed the tall young man with the smooth moves. In 2013, the Milwaukee Bucks chose Antetokounmpo with the 15th overall pick in the **NBA Draft**.

Antetokounmpo looks for an open teammate during a 2017 game.

In 2016, Bucks head coach Jason Kidd made a surprising decision. He told his players that Antetokounmpo would be the team's starting **point guard** in 2017. The Greek Freak has the skills to play the position. Yet he doesn't look much like a point guard.

Antetokounmpo reaches for the basket during a game against the Washington Wizards.

The average NBA point guard is about 6 feet 2 (1.8 m). Antetokounmpo is 6 feet 11 (2.1 m). His hands measure 12 inches (30 cm) from the base of his hand to the tip of his middle finger. That's longer than other NBA stars of similar height. Even tall basketball legends such as Wilt Chamberlain had smaller hands. Antetokounmpo's **wingspan** is 7 feet 3 (2.2 m). His long arms and hands help him reach balls before other players can.

Point guards need to be quick and **agile**. Some of Antetokounmpo's agility comes from working with his

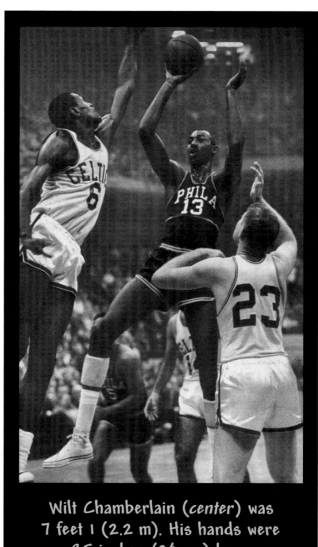

Wilt Chamberlain (center) was 7 feet 1 (2.2 m). His hands were 9.5 inches (24 cm) long.

father, who had played soccer in Nigeria. In Greece, he led his sons in soccer workouts to improve the quickness of their feet.

Antetokounmpo spends a lot of time in the gym practicing basketball and training his body. He works out every day, even after returning from a long trip with the team. Sometimes he works out after games. If his team lost, he may shoot baskets and replay the game in his mind late into the night.

Antetokounmpo lifts heavy weights to strengthen his legs. He jumps rope and uses stretchy bands to work up a sweat. He makes sure to do a variety of workouts to improve all of his muscles.

In 2016, the Bucks rewarded Antetokounmpo for his hard work with a new contract. The team agreed to pay him $100 million for the next four seasons. Antetokounmpo delayed signing the contract for four hours while he worked out.

Antetokounmpo practices shooting before a
2018 game in New York.

On the court, Antetokounmpo practices shooting from every angle and distance. He dribbles forward, steps quickly to his right, and shoots. Then he does the same move to the left. He practices driving to the basket and passing the ball at the last moment. He works hard to make the most of his height and long arms.

Antetokounmpo reaches for a dunk during a 2013 game.

Antetokounmpo poses for a photo shortly after joining the Bucks in 2013.

When Antetokounmpo came to the United States in 2013, he left his parents and brothers behind in Greece. They would eventually move to Milwaukee, but until then, the family used Skype to stay in touch. With the video service,

Antetokounmpo could even give his family a virtual tour of his apartment.

By 2014, Antetokounmpo's parents and brothers had joined him in Wisconsin. Since then, Antetokounmpo can often be found hanging out with them when he isn't playing basketball. They visit restaurants in Milwaukee and nearby Chicago to feast on their favorite foods. Sushi is especially high on Antetokounmpo's list. The brothers also have fun with games and dance parties.

Antetokounmpo (left) and his brother Thanasis played basketball in an event known as Antetokounbros Streetball in Greece in 2016.

Kostas Antetokounmpo holds off a defender in
a 2018 game at Dayton.

Can you imagine someone as tall as Antetokounmpo trying to hide? One of his favorite things to do is play laser tag. He says no one can see him when he stays low to the ground. He and his brothers also like to play paintball.

Alex began high school in Milwaukee in 2016. Kostas graduated in 2016 and went on to play basketball at the University of Dayton. Antetokounmpo often attends Alex's games. He shouts, cheers, and jumps up and down with excitement. "He teaches [his brothers] about basketball, about life, about priorities," said their father.

to honor their new country. They also gave them Nigerian names. Giannis's Nigerian name is Ougko.

The name Giannis Antetokounmpo is hard to say for many people who don't speak Greek and Nigerian. His name is pronounced **YAHN**-iss Ah-deh-toh-**KOON**-boh.

ESPN announcer Ryan Ruocco took lessons in Yoruba, a Nigerian language, to learn how to pronounce Antetokounmpo's name correctly.

Antetokounmpo (*right*) and his brother Thanasis
spoke about their achievements in 2017.

One of Antetokounmpo's priorities is giving back
to people in his area. Operation Dream is a group
in Milwaukee that helps boys in need. The group
provides a safe space where kids can hang out,
learn to overcome challenges, and plan for the
future. Antetokounmpo takes part in events with
Operation Dream. He tells boys about his journey to
NBA stardom and the importance of setting goals.

BUCK STAR

Antetokounmpo brings the ball down the court in 2016.

As soon as Antetokounmpo signed his huge new contract with the Bucks in 2016, fans started talking about 2021–2022. That's the NBA season after his contract ends. He'll be just 26 years old, and his services will be in high demand.

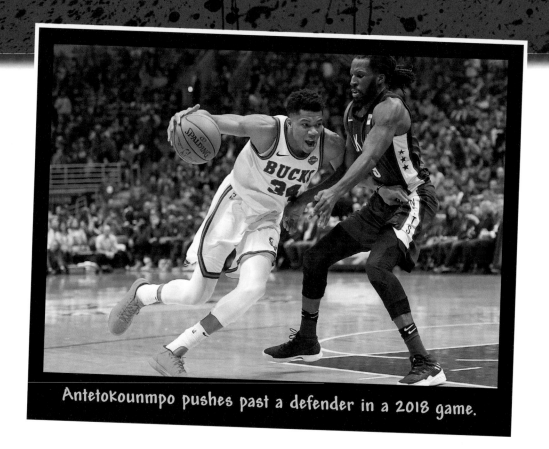
Antetokounmpo pushes past a defender in a 2018 game.

Some people are already guessing that he might move on from Milwaukee. But Antetokounmpo has stated that he loves the team and wants to stay.

No matter what happens, Bucks fans can enjoy the Greek Freak for the next few seasons at least. He gets better every year. His points-per-game average went from 6.8 as a **rookie** to 22.9 in 2016–2017. His rebounds and assists per game have gone up each season as well.

Antetokounmpo jumps for a shot during
the 2017 All-Star Game.

    By 2016–2017, he was a genuine NBA superstar.
A panel of sportswriters voted him the league's Most
Improved Player that season. He was also selected as
an All-Star Game starter for the first time.

The rise of Antetokounmpo has matched a rise in the fortunes of the Bucks. In his first season, the team had a terrible 15–67 record. Since then, Milwaukee has won at least 33 games each season and has been to the playoffs twice.

The next step for the Greek Freak is to help his team succeed in the playoffs. Good players must win championships to become great, and greatness is Antetokounmpo's goal. "I don't want to be a good player," he said. "I want to be a great one."

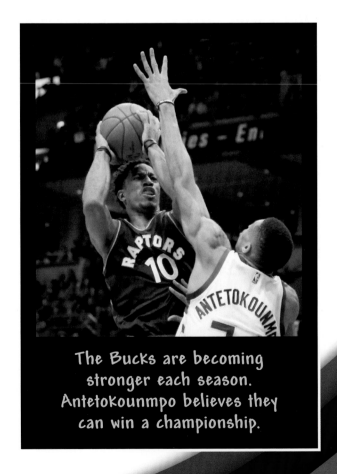

The Bucks are becoming stronger each season. Antetokounmpo believes they can win a championship.

All-Star Stats

Antetokounmpo's 2016–2017 season was one of the best in team history. His 1,832 points ranked in Milwaukee's top 10 of all time. Appearing on the same stats list as Kareem Abdul-Jabbar shows he's done something special. Abdul-Jabbar was voted one of the 50 Greatest Players in NBA History. Take a look at where Antetokounmpo's season ranked in team history.

Most Points by a Player in a Season in Milwaukee Bucks History

Player	Season	Points
Kareem Abdul-Jabbar	1971–1972	2,822
Kareem Abdul-Jabbar	1970–1971	2,596
Kareem Abdul-Jabbar	1969–1970	2,361
Kareem Abdul-Jabbar	1972–1973	2,292
Kareem Abdul-Jabbar	1973–1974	2,191
Michael Redd	2005–2006	2,028
Marques Johnson	1978–1979	1,972
Kareem Abdul-Jabbar	1974–1975	1,949
Terry Cummings	1984–1985	1,861
Giannis Antetokounmpo	2016–2017	1,832

Source Notes

[7] Associated Press, "Bucks Overwhelm Raptors, 104–77, Take 2–1 Series Lead," *ESPN,* April 20, 2017, http://www.espn.com/nba/recap?gameId=400950410.

[9] Jim Owczarski, "NBA Provides an Escape for Bucks Rookie Antetokounmpo," *OnMilwaukee*, October 22, 2013, https://onmilwaukee.com/sports/articles/giannisantetokounmpo.html?viewall=1.

[11] Joanna Kakissis, "NBA Rookie Wants to Bring Hope to Greece, and to Milwaukee," *NPR*, September 26, 2013, http://www.npr.org/2013/09/26/226268651/nbas-g-bo-wants-to-bring-hope-to-greece-and-to-milwaukee.

[21] "Hangin' with Giannis Antetokounmpo: A Revealing Portrait of a Close Family Man and Big Brother," NBPA, April 18, 2016, https://nbpa.com/hangin-with-giannis-antetokounmpo-a-revealing-portrait-of-a-close-family-man-and-big-brother.

[27] Adrian Wojnarowski, "From Street Vendor to Surging NBA Player, Greek Freak Living the American Dream," *Yahoo! Sports*, March 18, 2014, https://sports.yahoo.com/news/from-selling-sunglasses-on-street-to-nba-player-on-the-rise--greek-freak-living-the-american-dream-214309752.html.

Glossary

agile: able to move quickly and easily

assist: a pass to a teammate that results in a score

block: to strike the ball to prevent a score

contract: an agreement between a player and a team that states how much the player will be paid and for how long

NBA Draft: an event in which teams take turns choosing new players

playoffs: a series of games held to decide a champion

point guard: the player who leads a basketball team on offense

pro: something done for money that many people do for fun

rebounds: balls that bounce away from the basket after missed shots

rookie: a first-year player

scout: a person who judges the talents of athletes

wingspan: the distance from the tip of a player's hand to the tip of the other hand with the arms straight out

Further Information

Giannis Antetokounmpo
http://www.nba.com/players/giannis/antetokounmpo/203507

Gitlin, Marty. *Playing Pro Basketball*. Minneapolis: Lerner Publications, 2015.

Jr. NBA
https://jr.nba.com

Milwaukee Bucks
http://www.nba.com/bucks

Moussavi, Sam. *Milwaukee Bucks*. New York: AV2 by Weigl, 2016.

Savage, Jeff. *Basketball Super Stats*. Minneapolis: Lerner Publications, 2018.

Index

Photo Acknowledgments

Image credits: iStock.com/63151, (gold and silver stars); Stacy Revere/Getty Images, pp. 2, 13, 25; AP Photo/Morry Gash, pp. 4–5, 6; s-mart/Shutterstock.com, p. 8; Jamie McCarthy/Getty Images, p. 9; Wassilios Aswestopoulos/NurPhoto/Getty Images, p. 10; Matteo Marchi/Getty Images, pp. 11, 17; Mike Stobe/Getty Images, p. 12; Rob Carr/Getty Images, p. 14; George Silk/The LIFE Picture Collection/Getty Images, p. 15; Jacob Langston/Orlando Sentinel/Getty Images, p. 18; Nick Laham/Getty Images, p. 19; Ververidis Vasilis/Shutterstock.com, p. 20; Adam Lacy/Icon Sportswire/Getty Images, p. 21; Cindy Ord/Getty Images, p. 22; ELEFTHERIOS ELIS/AFP/Getty Images, p. 23; Mike McGinnis/Getty Images, p. 24; Ronald Martinez/Getty Images, p. 26; Dylan Buell/Getty Images, p. 27.

Cover: Stacy Revere/Getty Images; iStock.com/neyro2008 (motion lines).